Helping Kids Live Their Faith

service projects that make a difference

Mary Beth Jambor

RCL✝
Benziger®

a Kendall Hunt Company

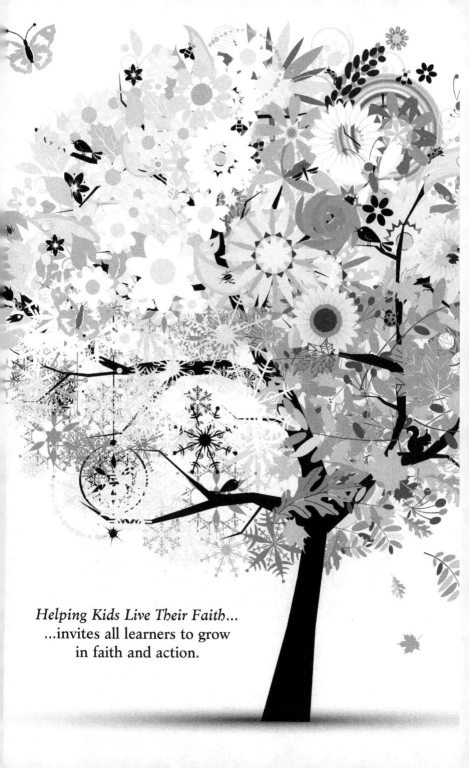

Helping Kids Live Their Faith...
...invites all learners to grow
in faith and action.

Cover and Interior Images: Thinkstock

Send all inquiries to:
RCL Benziger
8805 Governor's Hill Drive, Suite 400
Cincinnati, OH 45249

Telephone: 877-275-4725
Fax: 800-688-8356

Visit us at **RCLBenziger.com**

Printed in the United States of America.

441933   ISBN 978-1-5249-1933-7

7th Printing
January 2017

CONTENTS

INTRODUCTION

Helping Kids Live Their Faith: Service Projects That Make a Difference is written for you, the directors of religious education, youth ministers, catechists, teachers, volunteers, parents, and all who are involved in the religious formation of children and youth. Each of you has an essential role in handing on faith to our young people. You provide them with the opportunities to both learn about and live out their faith. You also serve as a model of faith. You help them see what it looks like to live a life of faith.

This book is organized in an easy-to-use format. The introduction explains the foundation on which the service project ideas are based and will help you understand how service is integral to the mission of the Church. It also offers suggestions for incorporating service into programs for children and youth.

Chapters 1 through 7 outline numerous service projects for young people of all ages. They are based on the seven principles of Catholic Social Teaching as outlined in 1998 by the United States Catholic Conference of Bishops in *Sharing Catholic Social Teaching: Challenges and Directions:* (1) Life and Dignity of the Human Person; (2) Call to Family, Community, and Participation; (3) Solidarity; (4) Option for the Poor and Vulnerable; (5) Dignity of Work and the Rights of Workers; (6) Rights and Responsibilities; and (7) Care of Creation.

Chapter 8 addresses peace. In a society where some forms of violence are commonplace, and some become acceptable norms, we need to help young people recognize how violence and hatred can permeate our culture. We need to give them the tools to live as peacemakers and the opportunity to make a difference in the world.

Chapter 9 looks at fundraising through the lens of our service mission. Here you will find creative fundraising ideas that can simultaneously raise money for your youth service projects and provide a service to the parish or community.

Chapter 10 contains a list of dos and don'ts. Whether you are a novice or experienced at organizing service projects with youth, take time to look at this chapter. It will help you avoid common mishaps and oversights.

This book concludes with a list of agencies, organizations, and offices. These can be valuable resources as you plan and prepare service projects.

SERVICE AND THE MISSION
OF THE CHURCH

The mission of the Church makes clear that service is integral to Catholics. The Church's mission is threefold. It includes Word, worship, and service. We live out the mission of Word by reading Scripture and spreading the Good News of Jesus Christ. We carry out our mission of worship as we participate in liturgies and communal prayer. We live out the mission of service as we serve one another and the Church.

The Catholic Church has proclaimed its social teaching for more than one hundred years, beginning with *Rerum Novarum* in 1891. As recently as 1998, the United States Catholic

Conference of Bishops published *Sharing Catholic Social Teaching: Challenges and Directions.* This document summarizes the history of Catholic Social Teaching. Seven social justice principles emerge and the bishops conclude by offering challenges and directions to parishes. Their goal is to encourage parishes to broaden, deepen, and strengthen Catholic Social Teaching in Catholic schools and parish religious education programs.

Take time to teach young people about the mission of the Church and our long history of Catholic Social Teaching. As you do this, you will help them understand that service is not an extracurricular activity. We are baptized into the common priesthood, and by virtue of our Baptism, we are called to carry out the ministries of Jesus Christ in the world today. Service is essential to this call.

BEFORE YOU BEGIN

As you begin to plan, develop, and implement service projects with young people, you will want to give adequate time and attention to your choices.

In choosing projects, keep in mind the ages of the children with whom you are working. Be sure that the project is developmentally appropriate for the group. Ask yourself if the children are physically, mentally, and socially capable of participating in and completing the project.

Choose projects that work well with a group of young people. Serving in community with others is always beneficial. The old adage "Many hands make the work lighter" holds true for a number of reasons.

1. A group can cut the time a large project may take.

2. Children may draw courage from their peers when they find themselves in unfamiliar settings.

3. Working together will help build community and friendships among the group members.

Also choose projects that vary in their circle of influence. For example, if one project serves the parish, perhaps the next project can serve people in another country. Help the children understand that they can serve people in their families, their parish, their neighborhoods, their communities, around their country, and in other countries of the world.

Be sure to take time to both prepare young people for a project and debrief afterward. Here are some simple suggestions:

Preparation

1. Tell the children about the people they will be serving.

2. Help the children understand the needs of those they will serve.

3. Provide an opportunity for the children to share what they hope for and what they may be concerned about.

4. Make your expectations clear. Include your behavior expectations.

5. Make the agency's or organization's expectations clear.

Debriefing

1. Ask the children what they learned about the people they served.

2. Ask the children what they learned about themselves.

3. Give the children the opportunity to talk about how they felt while they were doing the project. Were they nervous? Did they become more comfortable? Did they have a good time?

4. Ask the children to explain how they feel they made a difference in the lives of the people they served.

5. Ask the children to share what worked well.

6. Ask the children to share what did not work well or what may have been frustrating. Give them a chance to share their suggestions for improvement.

7. If appropriate, provide an opportunity for the children to share stories of their service experience with their families and the parish or school community.

Finally, encourage the children to get involved. Help them understand that each of us plays an essential role in our Church. We cannot stand around and point out to people what needs to or could be done. Help the young people see that if they don't do it, it won't get done!

CHAPTER 1

LIFE AND DIGNITY
OF THE HUMAN PERSON

As Catholics, we believe that each and every one of us is created in the image and likeness of God. Based on this belief, the Catholic Church asserts that all human life is sacred. Our belief in the sanctity of human life and the dignity of the human person provides the foundation of a moral vision of society. Upon this foundation rests all Catholic Social Teaching.

In our society today, we may hear of some who promote a theory of survival of the fittest. Some use arguments about quality of life to support euthanasia and abortion as acts of mercy. As believers, we are called to reach out to the weak, the dying, the elderly, and the unborn with compassion. Abortion and euthanasia are not acts of mercy. Instead we believe our acts of mercy involve sharing Christ's love with those most in need.

" We believe that every person is precious, that people are more important than things, and that the measure of every institution is whether it threatens or enhances the life and dignity of the human person (*Sharing Catholic Social Teaching: Challenges and Directions* 4). "

The Elderly

For many years, our parish has enjoyed a close relationship with our local nursing home where the staff always welcomes parish volunteers of all ages.

When I was in sixth grade, our catechist loved to sing. She taught us to sing some of the residents' favorite songs. During our visits, the residents filled the cafeteria and sang with us. Afterward, we would stroll through the hallways and share our music with those who were unable to come to the cafeteria.

Currently, our middle school youth group visits the care center on a regular schedule to play Bingo with the residents. The kids call the game, make certain the residents hear the numbers called, and distribute prizes. They also help any residents who need special assistance.

The residents look forward to spending time with the youth. After a little initial discomfort, the young people can see what a difference they make in the residents' lives. Our middle school youth enjoy Bingo at the care center so much that we have doubled our number of scheduled visits for the upcoming year!

Serving the Elderly

1. Build bird feeders and birdhouses for seniors to hang in their yards. Find a church member who can teach young people how to make a birdhouse or feeder from a simple pattern. Explain the project to a local building supply store and request material donations.

2. Make homemade treats for the homebound. This is a great project around the holidays. Thanks to the treats you make, the homebound will have treats to share with their holiday visitors. Deliver the treats personally or give them to volunteers who visit the homebound in your community. If you choose to send the treats with other volunteers, be sure to include a card from your class or group.

3. Interview longtime members of your parish and put together a booklet of their stories and recollections. Make copies of the booklet and share it with the whole community.

4. Record Sunday Mass and other special parish and school gatherings. Make copies of the recordings to give to the homebound.

5. Encourage families to take a senior grocery shopping or on other family outings and errands.

6. Arrange to lead Bingo at a nursing home, senior center, or senior housing complex. Bring healthful treats or small unwrapped gifts for prizes. Be sure to speak loudly and clearly while calling the game. Have a few young people at each table to assist the players.

7. Arrange to visit a nursing home, senior center, or senior housing complex to play games with the residents. Games like cards, checkers, and chess provide a one-on-one opportunity to get to know the seniors.

8. Offer to assist the elderly in wrapping their Christmas gifts or addressing their Christmas cards. Many seniors have difficulty with vision and arthritis, which can make doing these holiday tasks difficult.

9. Arrange to help seniors with holiday makeovers. Many seniors will have family visiting over the holidays and want to look their best. Volunteer to help them with fixing hair, trimming or polishing nails, and shaving.

10. Arrange to visit a senior facility to lead a songfest. Learn some songs from when the seniors were young; they will love to sing them!

11. Bring flowers to an elderly person. You will let them know that they are special today and you may help them remember a time when a loved one brought them flowers. Ask them to share their memories with you.

12. Plant flowers and help tend the grounds of a senior facility. Residents who were once avid gardeners take great pleasure in enjoying such gardens.

21

13. Read and write letters for seniors. Failing vision and finger dexterity make reading and writing difficult for some elderly. Help them keep up with their correspondence.

14. Volunteer at a senior facility to help seniors learn to use the variety of digital devices available to them. Many facilities provide various digital devices, but do not have the staff to teach the seniors how to use them.

15. Host a senior prom. Serve healthful treats and play music from your guests' era. Dance with those who can, and encourage everyone to move to the music. Be sure that hosts and hostesses dress well for this special occasion.

16. Host a holiday party. Decorate, serve treats, play games, and include music to celebrate any holiday. You might even like to help the seniors make a craft.

17. Provide meals-on-wheels to seniors on days that agencies do not provide them or volunteer with your local Meals on Wheels organization.

18. Offer rides to church for seniors who do not drive or those who choose not to drive in poor weather. Your parish priest or pastoral minister can identify people who are in need of transportation.

19. Invite a senior to sit with you at church. They may long for the days when they attended church with their spouse or family. For those newly widowed, attending Mass alone can be a difficult adjustment.

20. Make prayer cards or holiday cards for seniors. Deliver them to senior facilities or ask those who visit the homebound to deliver the cards.

21. Call nursing homes, care facilities, senior day-care centers, and senior centers to find out how you can help.

22. Adopt a grandparent. Seniors make excellent companions!

23. Become a prayer partner with a senior.

Serving Expectant Parents and New Parents

1. Organize a diaper coupon collection. Distribute the coupons to parents in your church, or donate them to a food pantry or ministry to single parents.

2. Babysit for new parents. Even watching a baby for a short time at home so that a new mom can relax and take a bath or nap is helpful.

3. Host a baby shower for expectant parents in your church. Play games, bring gifts, and pray with the parents.

4. Create baby layettes or care packages for new parents. Include books, diapers, blankets, onesies, and other necessities. Distribute the items to single moms, food pantries, family shelters, area churches, or your diocesan Catholic Charities adoption services ministry.

5. Organize people to take turns providing meals for new parents during their first week at home with a new baby. Taking care of a newborn is tiring, and a tasty homemade meal is appreciated.

6. Pray for expectant parents and their unborn baby throughout the entire pregnancy. Send cards every few weeks to let the parents know you are still praying for them.

7. Organize a collection for your diocesan Catholic Charities adoption services ministry. Contact your local Catholic Charities office to determine specific items needed. Items that may be requested include baby furniture, diapers, clothes, formula, and blankets.

8. Organize a maternity clothes collection. Make the clothing available to expectant moms in your parish or distribute them to your local Catholic Charities office. To locate the Catholic Charities office nearest you, go to catholiccharitiesusa.org.

The Intellectually and Developmentally Challenged

About a dozen intellectually and developmentally challenged adults live in the Northeast Residence, a group home in our community. For nearly twenty years, the Northeast Residence was housed in our vacated parish convent. A few years ago, the Northeast Residence purchased a large home nearby. The home is less institutional and better meets the needs of the residents and staff.

When the Northeast Residence changed locations, the parish Respect Life Committee very deliberately maintained our ties with the facility. During this time, our middle school youth began providing a Christmas party for the residents with assistance from the Respect Life Committee.

25

The Northeast Residence staff provides us with a list of names and gift ideas. The middle schoolers each donate a small amount of money. Then a couple of youth volunteers shop for the gifts. At the party, which is held at the facility, the Respect Life Committee serves treats and the middle schoolers distribute gifts to all the residents. And of course, we all sing Christmas carols together.

Serving Persons who are Intellectually and Developmentally Challenged

1. Get involved with Special Olympics. This organization utilizes both long-term and short-term volunteers. They need coaches to teach and train athletes. For the big events such as track meets, each athlete needs a host to guide them through the events of the day. For more information, go to specialolympics.org.

2. Pair a child with special needs and a child who can serve as a friend and advocate in your parish religious education program. Both children will benefit from working together.

3. Develop a relationship with a group home in your community. Visit the facility on a regular basis to play games with residents, or host parties at the facility on special occasions.

4. Find out about camps or organizations in your area that serve persons who are intellectually or developmentally challenged. Contact the facilities and discover how you can help. Facilities often provide training for volunteers who are willing to donate their time. Your diocese may have an office which specializes in ministry to those with special needs. They can also be a resource for local agencies in need of volunteers.

5. Raise funds to send a person in your community with a mental health disability to a summer camp.

6. Pair a child with special needs and a child who can serve as a friend when participating in special youth events and outings. Make sure that the parents of a child with special needs know that the child will be partnered with a friend during the event.

The Physically Disabled

Our senior high youth group has made bathrooms accessible and has built wheelchair ramps. When modifying a bathroom, we must make certain we determine the needs. Does the resident want a nonskid floor and tub? Or does a wheelchair need to pass through the doorway? Sometimes accessible can mean safer, not necessarily wheelchair accessible.

Building a wheelchair ramp requires precision. We need to construct a ramp according to specifications which determine the percent grade of the incline and dimensions of corners. I find that high school youth have exceptional math skills and can easily figure out a plan for a ramp.

Serving Persons with Physical Disabilities

1. Help with physical therapy. Those with severe physical disabilities need numerous hours of physical therapy everyday in their homes. Get involved with a team of volunteers and commit to helping with therapy sessions for an hour a week.

28

2. Set up partners to host persons with physical disabilities at church events. Be sure the hosts are aware of the location of accessible entrances and restrooms as well as any specific needs their partner may have.

3. Help those with poor vision with reading and writing. Paying bills and responding to mail can be made easier with a little assistance.

4. Offer to make phone calls for those who have difficulty hearing.

5. Make someone's home accessible. Build wheelchair ramps and install bathroom support rails.

6. If your church is not accessible to persons with disabilities, raise funds to make it accessible.

Those With Terminal Illness

One of the largest events in our town each summer is the Relay for Life. The Relay for Life is a fundraiser for the American Cancer Society. Participants register in teams and team members find people to sponsor them. The teams commit to having at least one member running a local path or track all night long.

Each year, the Relay for Life event in our community sells about 16,000 luminaries to honor cancer survivors or memorialize persons who have died of cancer. Our middle schoolers help prepare luminaries all year long. Throughout the year, we fold bags and stamp them "In memory of _____" or "In honor of _____." On the day of the relay, youth groups around the area volunteer to place the bags around the track and fill them with a candle and sand.

This year, many members of our high-school youth group registered as a team and participated in the relay.

Serving Persons with Terminal Illness

1. Visit someone who is in hospice care. Listen to their stories. Offer to read to them.

2. Become a prayer partner for someone who is terminally ill. Your pastor or pastoral minister can give you the name of someone for whom to pray.

3. Make cards with comforting messages for those who are terminally ill. You might like to include Scripture quotes.

4. Participate in fundraisers for organizations such as those listed below that fund research and patient costs for terminal illnesses.
   - AIDS Healthcare Foundation (aidshealthorg)
   - American Heart Association (heart.org)
   - American Cancer Society (cancer.org)
   - Cystic Fibrosis Foundation (cff.org)
   - Multiple Sclerosis Foundation (msfocus.org)

5. Contact a hospice in your area to find out about volunteer opportunities.

6. Contact a hospice in your area and offer to host a food drive.

Those in Prison

Our children make seasonal cards for prison inmates. However, we have learned that we must determine from prison staff what materials we can use to make the cards, since some craft materials are not allowed inside the prison.

Inmates do appreciate such cards from children. We receive a note of gratitude from the inmates every time!

Serving Persons in Prison

1. Organize a book collection for donations to the prison library.

2. Write letters and cards to inmates. Prison staff can make certain that children correspond only with inmates who are not a threat to the children. Remember that children should sign their first names only, and share no personal information in their letters and cards.

3. Make Christmas stockings for inmates.

4. Spend time at a juvenile center and lead recreational activities. Juvenile center staff can offer suggestions regarding appropriate activities.

5. Organize a toiletry collection for inmates or those moving to halfway houses. Because of the expense involved, prisons and halfway houses are often unable to provide such items.

6. Contact your parish or diocesan Prison Ministry to find out how you can get involved.

CHAPTER 2

CALL TO FAMILY, COMMUNITY, AND PARTICIPATION

We are called to live out our faith in our families and in our community. The opportunities for getting involved and making a difference in the lives of those around us are limitless!

While our society often promotes individualism, the Catholic Church teaches that we grow and achieve fulfillment in community (see *Sharing Catholic Social Teaching: Challenges and Directions* 5).

In the Parish and School

1. Help with parish and school mailings and other large, labor-intensive projects. Folding, stuffing, labeling, and stamping a bulk mailing can be an overwhelming task for one person alone. Or it can become an opportunity to visit, listen to music, catch up with friends, and help the parish and school at the same time!

2. Make publicity posters for parish and school events. Invite the children and youth to put their digital skills to use to create both digital and print media to publicize events.

3. Get involved in liturgical ministries. Find out your diocesan and parish guidelines regarding youth involvement in liturgical ministries. Encourage the young people, where appropriate, to serve as lectors, extraordinary ministers of Holy Communion, music ministers, altar servers, Liturgy of the Word With Children assistants, ministers of hospitality, or gift bearers.

4. As a youth group, take responsibility for all the hospitality ministries at one Mass a month. As children get older, they may prefer to serve with their peers as well as with their families.

5. Set up grade-level buddies. For example, pair a first-grade group with a fourth-grade group and assign each person a buddy. Throughout the year, bring the groups together for art projects, service projects, and celebrations. Young children thrive on special attention from older children. Older children feel good about themselves when they are helpful.

6. Organize prayer partners for children preparing for the Sacraments. Make cards with the first names of the children on them. Put them in a basket and place the basket near the entrance of the church. Invite parishioners to take a name and pray for the child throughout his or her preparation.

7. Create a prayer network. Provide a box where parishioners deposit their written prayer requests. On a regular basis, distribute a list of prayer requests to those who choose to serve the community through prayer. Many of the youth may even want to regularly pray in response to these prayer requests.

8. Make welcome cards for children and adults who are initiated into the Church through Baptism and the RCIA (Rite of Christian Initiation of Adults). Arrange with the parish office to include the cards in the envelopes with the certificates.

9. Provide child care at parish events. This service makes it more possible for parents of young children to attend events.

10. Make luminaries for Christmas Eve Mass. Assemble the luminaries ahead of time. Then invite youth or families to take responsibility for setting up and cleaning up the luminaries before and after Mass.

11. Invite a friend or relative to a Mass or parish event. If you think your parish is wonderful, you can serve by helping someone else get connected to your community.

12. Offer to clean the church. Keeping the church tidy inside and out is a big job. Many hands can make the work quick and fun. Besides, the church belongs to us, the parish members. It is up to all of us to take care of our church.

13. Set up ministry mentors. Give young people an opportunity to find out more about a ministry before making a commitment. Ask volunteers to mentor young people who are interested in getting more involved. The young people can shadow volunteer ministers or find out what people find most rewarding about their ministry. This is a good activity for those preparing for Confirmation.

14. Develop a plan for welcoming new parishioners to your parish. The plan could include handing out welcome cards, inviting young people to youth events, or hosting a picnic where new parishioners can meet other parishioners.

15. Plan and host an all ages, alcohol-free New Year's Eve party. The party could include music, dancing, potluck dinner or desserts, games, or raffles.

16. Invite a person who attends church alone to sit with you. Single adults, those newly divorced, or the elderly may feel uncomfortable attending Mass alone. Invite someone to join you and your family.

17. Help families move. Offer to watch the children while parents pack boxes and supervise the move. Prepare meals for the family. Let them know you will miss them.

In the Community

Each summer, White Bear Lake, Minnesota area churches team up for *Summer Stretch. Summer Stretch* is a summer program for middle and high school youth. One day each week youth gather in the morning

37

for prayer and service activities, and spend the afternoon participating in fun and social/recreational events.

Hundreds of young people participate each summer. Many service sites benefit from our youth each week. And by the end of the summer, young people have experienced eight different service activities.

People who are out and about on *Summer Stretch* days in White Bear Lake cannot help but notice all the kids in *Summer Stretch* T-shirts. The youth tend community gardens, help with summer maintenance projects in the local schools, provide activities for young children, and much more!

The youth ministers of the different churches appreciate the opportunity to minister as a team. We each take responsibility for a separate piece of the programming responsibilities. The youth enjoy participating with their friends as well as meeting new friends, regardless of church affiliation.

Getting Involved in the Community

1. Team up with other churches in your community for youth service projects. Young people will see how they can make a difference when all denominations work together. Be sure to provide time for socializing.

2. Paint murals over graffiti. Talk to city officials to get permission. Find out if a local hardware or paint store can provide the materials.

3. Arrange with a local elementary school or after-school program to host after-school activities for children in need. Invite youth from the school and parish to help the younger children prepare puppet shows or design their own three-ring circus. Also consider teaching crafts, reading books, and playing games and sports.

4. Welcome new students to school. Invite them to eat lunch with you and your friends. Also, help them find their way around the school and the community.

5. Volunteer at a local library. Libraries are always looking for people to read to children and to shelve books.

6. Help with your community festival. A youth group can set up tables or chairs, post No Parking signs, serve food, or take responsibility for cleanup. Talk to officials or the local Chamber of Commerce to find out how to get involved.

7. Call the local grocery store to volunteer. Suggest the opportunity to bag groceries and help people to their cars at the grocery store. Parents with small children and seniors will welcome assistance. Grocery stores will also appreciate the opportunity to provide customers with extra hospitality.

8. Arrange to help with cleaning and grounds work at your school and parish over the summer. Most parishes and schools save their biggest maintenance projects for the summer months. Young people can help move furniture, paint or repair playground equipment, clean pews and hymnal racks, or clean windows. Call the pastor, the principal, the school or parish maintenance supervisor, or the local district maintenance and grounds office to find out ways you can help.

CHAPTER 3

SOLIDARITY

" Catholic social teaching proclaims that we are our brothers' and sisters' keepers, wherever they live. We are one human family, whatever our national, racial, ethnic, economic, and ideological differences (*Sharing Catholic Social Teaching: Challenges and Directions* 5). **"**

Solidarity means "to stand with." As Catholics, we believe that solidarity means loving our neighbor, and we realize it is a global responsibility. As believers, we must not allow ourselves to slide into cultural norms and become indifferent or isolationist. We must keep ourselves informed and look for ways we can make a difference and stand with those in need.

Newly Arrived

A number of times each year, I receive calls from people who have a bed they no longer need. These families prefer to donate their beds rather than to sell them. In fact, most families donate any bedding they have along with the bed.

For families entering the country, beds and bedding are expensive. Many live for months or longer sleeping on the floor.

Youth can pick up beds, bedding, and sofa beds from families who have donations and bring them to agencies for distribution to families in need.

Helping the Newly Arrived

1. Contact your diocesan Refugee and Migration Services office to inquire about the specific needs of those being served and how you can help meet those needs.

2. Contact your parish or diocesan Refugee and Migration Services ministry to see if there is a need for new bedding and/or beds and sofa beds. Beds and bedding can be among the most expensive items needed by immigrants and refugees.

3. Collect clothing for your climate. Often immigrants and refugees arrive with only the clothes they are wearing or clothing unsuited to the climate of their new home.

4. Volunteer to provide transportation. It may take many months for immigrants to obtain a driver's license.

5. Teach a newly arrived family about the public transportation system in your community.

6. Offer to help a newly arrived family with errands. Older youth or families can help family members learn where to go, how to get there, and whom to contact.

7. Offer hospitality and friendship. The most important gift we can share with immigrants is our love and care.

8. Donate religious gifts to immigrants. Catholic and Christian families will appreciate gifts of crucifixes, religious pictures, or rosaries for their homes.

9. Collect photo albums. Distribute them to families so that they can place pictures of their children in the albums.

10. Help newly arrived classmates at school. Offer to guide the new students to classes, through lunch, and to the administrative and counseling offices. Invite them to join extracurricular activities.

11. Offer activities for migrant children. Youth can read books, tutor, teach crafts, organize sports and games, or lead religion classes.

Disaster Relief

On a regular basis, we place a glass bowl
on a table near our baptismal font at church.
In the bowl, we collect donations for a variety
of causes, depending on current needs in our
community and in the world.

We have collected for causes such
as flood relief and war refugees.
When the glass bowl appears,
people always look to read where their
donations will go.

Caring for Victims of Natural Disasters

1. Go to Catholic Relief Services (crs.org) or the
   American Red Cross (redcross.org) Web sites to
   see what materials and donations are needed for
   disaster relief. Collect monies and/or matierals
   for donation.

2. Take part in flood relief efforts by making sand
   bags, shoveling mud out of homes, and cleaning
   homes and yards.

3. Walk on farm fields after a tornado or severe storm.
   The fields need to be searched for valuable items
   and cleared of debris. Form teams to walk the fields
   side-by-side.

4. Contact your local homeless shelter and offer to collect teddy bears, blankets, backpacks, and basic supplies for homeless children in your area. Distribute also to fire and police departments or the local American Red Cross Chapter.

5. Contact your local chapter of the American Red Cross to ask about donating bottled water for local and national volunteers and victims of disasters.

6. Provide a basket in the common areas of the church for donations anytime disaster happens. Eventually, members of your parish will develop a habit of checking for the basket each time they come for Mass. Be sure to place a sign near the basket that describes where the funds will be sent.

7. Host a shower for a family who lost their home in a fire. Invite parish members to bring practical gifts such as kitchen utensils, clothing, toiletries, towels, blankets, groceries, and gift cards for groceries, gasoline, and local restaurants.

8. Contact local transportation businesses to assess their ability to help deliver donations such as bottled water and personal care items to victims of natural disasters in this country.

Missions and Poverty Abroad

1. Go to the Catholic Relief Services Web site (crs.org) to determine the areas of greatest need and donations needed right now, today. CRS works in over 90 countries and serves more than 100 million people each year.

2. Sponsor a child, a student, or an aging adult in one of twenty countries throughout the world through Unbound (unbound.org). This international nonprofit ministry, founded by lay Catholics, currently has over 250,000 sponsors serving over 300,000 people in need. Sponsors and those they serve maintain contact through letters, photos, and e-mail.

3. Donate livestock. Heifer International (HPI) uses donations to provide livestock, seeds, or training to families in need throughout the world. To find out more about their mission and ministry, go to heifer.org.

4. Collect donations for Oxfam International. Oxfam International (oxfam.org), including OxfamAmerica (oxfamamerica.org) is currently working in more than 90 countries to create lasting solutions to poverty, hunger, and social injustice. Visit Oxfam's Web site to learn more about their work or to make a donation.

CHAPTER 4

OPTION FOR THE POOR
AND VULNERABLE

Since the Second Vatican Council, the Catholic Church has established that the needs of the poor must come first. In Matthew 25:35–36, Jesus instructs us on how to care for the poor and vulnerable:

> "For I was hungry and you gave me food, I was thirsty and you gave me drink, a stranger and you welcomed me, naked and you clothed me, ill and you cared for me, in prison and you visited me."

In General

We have two collections that our parish welcomes year after year. One is a shoe collection. Anytime children outgrow their shoes, they can bring their shoes to the parish office.

About once a month, volunteers deliver the shoes to local shelters. Many children outgrow their shoes before they wear out. Both parents and kids welcome the opportunity to donate their shoes rather than throw them away.

Families also look forward to our after-Christmas winter clothing drive. By January, families know what winter clothes no longer fit their children. Also, Christmas has come and gone. New jackets and sweaters may take the place of clothing that can now be donated.

Serving the Poor and Vulnerable

1. Arrange to serve a meal at a soup kitchen or shelter. Some shelters provide the food for you to prepare and serve, while other shelters may ask you to furnish the food. Check with the shelter to find out their volunteer requirements, such as age, adult/child ratio, attire, and food preparation regulations.

2. Arrange to visit a shelter. If possible, talk to guests, listen to their stories, and offer to play cards or board games. Staff at the shelter can offer tips on preparing for the visit and interacting with guests.

3. Contact the head of your parish or local food pantry to find out if there are particular food items they need. Organize a food drive to help meet the need.

4. Organize a coat and mitten collection for your parish or local outreach to children in need. Fall and after Christmas are good times to hold these drives. Many children outgrow their winter clothes each year or replace them at Christmas time. Attach mittens and gloves to keep pairs together.

5. Organize clothing collections as the seasons change. These are the times of year that people go through their closets. You will make donating easier for people while providing donations for those in need.

6. Organize a shoe and sock collection. Those who are homeless often suffer from foot problems. Shelters often provide foot baths. However, clean socks and shoes are always in demand.

7. Explore ways to volunteer at your parish or local food pantry. Donations need to be gathered and organized. Food also needs to be packaged for distribution.

8. Volunteer at a local food bank. The Feeding America network is a nationwide network of food banks working together to provide food for families in need. To learn more about Feeding America, or to find out how to volunteer, go to feedingamerica.org.

9. Make homemade desserts for shelters that offer free meals.

10. Make fleece blankets for the homeless. These are simple enough for children and youth to make, too. Distribute them to shelters in your area.

11. Purchase food with all the trimmings for a holiday meal sponsored by your parish or a local homeless or emergency shelter. Holiday meals can be costly, and low-income families will appreciate your generosity.

12. Organize a donation of used cars. Engage the help of local auto mechanic students and technicians in order to repair the cars. Then donate them to the St. Vincent de Paul Auto Donation Program (yes-svdp.org). Repair and donate them.

13. Organize an all-night sleep-out to raise homelessness awareness in your community. Talk to city officials to arrange permission for the sleep-out to take place in a park or public space. Remember, sleeping bags and tents are not allowed. Only cardboard boxes are permitted. Post informational flyers throughout the area inviting people to visit your temporary homeless community.

Children in Need

Young children love to celebrate their birthdays! In our parish, we provide children with the opportunity to help children in need celebrate their birthdays too. All year round we collect cake mixes, frosting, candles, and small toys. As supplies accumulate, we assemble birthday boxes. Volunteers deliver the boxes to local food pantries and shelters. Our kids feel good about themselves when they realize they can help other children feel special on their birthdays.

Serving Children in Need

1. Organize a children's book drive. Donate the books to area shelters or libraries, churches, and schools in low-income areas.

2. Collect used and new bikes and toys. Don't forget outdoor toys like balls and jump ropes. If necessary, repair them before donating them. Deliver the donations to shelters, community centers, or churches in low-income areas.

3. Collect new and used school supplies. The end of the school year is a great time for this collection. As children pack up their lockers and desks, invite them to donate the unused portion of notebooks, markers, crayons, colored pencils, pencils, and pens. Or, as children prepare for a new school year, invite them to purchase items to donate. Deliver the donations to schools and churches in low-income areas.

4. Make special treats for children living in a homeless or family shelter. Make candy treat bags or decorate cookies and cupcakes. These kinds of treats are a rare contribution for children in need. The treats will be appreciated and will help the children know that others care for them.

5. Make baby kits for shelters. Collect items such as formula, diapers, washcloths, baby bath soap, baby lotion, and wipes. Distribute the care packages to local shelters and food pantries.

6. Make birthday boxes to help children in need celebrate their birthdays. Collect cake mixes, frosting, candles, and small toys appropriate for both boys and girls. Decorate bakery cake boxes and fill them with birthday items. Keep all ages of children in mind. Distribute the birthday boxes to local shelters and food pantires.

7. Collect inexpensive games and toys for local homeless and emergency shelters. Suggestions include decks of cards, crayons, bubbles, balls, jacks, jump ropes, coloring books, and books. Distribute the donations to local shelters and transitional housing facilities.

8. Organize an adopt-a-family program at Christmas. Find out the ages, sizes, and needs of families in need and give them to people who will be providing the gifts. If you do not have the donors wrap the presents, you might like to ask others to donate gift wrap paper. Most families in need will want to remain anonymous.

Be sure to respect their confidentiality. Parish staff, members of your local St. Vincent de Paul Society, food pantries, and shelters may be able to suggest possible recipients.

9. Make toys for children. Invite volunteers to teach youth how to make a few toys. Invite donations of materials. Distribute the toys to shelters, food pantries, and low-income churches.

10. Arrange to host a picnic or a party for children living in a shelter or transitional housing facility. Plan games and activities. Provide and serve special treats.

CHAPTER 5

DIGNITY OF WORK
AND THE RIGHTS OF WORKERS

" Work is more than a way to make a living; it is a form of continuing participation in God's creation. If the dignity of work is to be protected, then basic rights of workers must be respected. Respecting these rights promotes an economy that protects human life, defends human rights, and advances the well-being of all (*Sharing Catholic Social Teaching: Challenges and Directions* 5). **"**

As Catholic consumers, we are called to inform ourselves about the working conditions of people who make the products we purchase. We must also treat all people in service careers with respect.

Respecting Those Who Serve Our Country

During the Gulf War, many of our parishioners had friends and family who were sent to the Persian Gulf. For a few weeks we placed a note in the parish bulletin letting people know that if they had loved ones in the Gulf, we would send cards to them.

Quickly, the addresses poured in. We told the children a little bit about each person and provided them with materials for making cards.

Every person who received cards wrote back to us. They told about life in the Persian Gulf and how they missed home and their families. Some sent pictures of the planes they flew and the tents where they lived. One man even came to visit the children after the war.

58

Developing a
Social Conscience

Most high-school students have more disposable income than any other age group. Also during these years, young people are developing a social conscience. This is a perfect time to invite kids to investigate what types of labor conditions and businesses they support with their dollars.

Our young people discovered that from clothing to soccer balls, manufacturers utilize child labor camps in third-world countries. Once they informed each other about their findings, they committed to patronizing only businesses who followed particular labor regulations.

Serving Those Who Serve Us

1. Learn about retailers who are committed to promoting safe and healthy working conditions for all people. For more information, go to Fair Trade USA (fairtradeusa.org).

2. Arrange to host a teacher appreciation breakfast or cookies and cider for teachers after school.

3. Order pizzas for the school maintenance staff to enjoy while you take responsibility for the cafeteria setup and cleanup for a day.

4. Arrange to serve hot chocolate to school bus drivers as they drop off students at school. If possible, serve them on a cold winter morning.

5. Leave treats for your mail carrier in the mailbox. If you live in a warm climate, a bottle of water would make an appropriate treat.

6. When a person in a service position is exceptional, let his or her boss know!

7. Offer to help teachers, parish and school staff, and others with projects.

8. Write letters to military personnel who are away from their families. Put a note in the parish bulletin requesting names and addresses of those who would appreciate a letter.

9. Bring flowers to the school administrative assistant to have on her or his desk. Flowers will show how much you appreciate her or him.

10. Make thank-you cards for the pastor. Thank him for something specific. You might even consider using Scripture quotations on the cards.

CHAPTER 6

RIGHTS AND
RESPONSIBILITIES

❝ The Catholic tradition teaches that human dignity can be protected and a healthy community can be achieved only if human rights are protected and responsibilities are met. . . . Corresponding to these rights are duties and responsibilities— to one another, to our families, and to the larger society (*Sharing Catholic Social Teaching: Challenges and Directions* 5). **❞**

As Catholics, we are called to act in order to ensure that the rights of all people are protected. Begin by naming those who suffer from injustice. Then consider how to act.

Random Acts of Kindness

Youth in our parish offer a "Random Acts of Kindness" day each spring. We help elderly parishioners and community members with all sorts of spring cleanup chores. We trim shrubs, rake leaves, prepare gardens, and spread mulch. We also stain decks, wash windows, and move furniture from storage onto patios.

To find people who need assistance, our pastor and parish nurse provide us with a list of people to contact. We also call people who have lost a spouse in the last year. To make certain that we don't miss anyone, we also advertise our free service in the parish bulletin.

Each year, participation has grown. The first year we helped a dozen residents. This year, more than fifty volunteers helped nearly thirty residents!

We divide into work crews of about five: four youth and one adult. The adults provide transportation and assure the participants' safety. Each crew works at two or sometimes three homes.

Residents enjoy our company as much as they appreciate our hard work. Some call me in advance to find out what kind of soda or snacks the kids like. Others send thank-you cards and pictures afterward. The kids enjoy hearing the residents' stories about how our town or church used to be.

At the end of the day, we gather for dinner and share stories about our experiences.

Group Workcamp

High-school youth in our parish have participated in Workcamp for the past six years. For many young people Workcamp is a formative and life-changing experience.

Workcamp is an ecumenical youth camp organized through Group Publishing. Every summer, Group offers over fifty camps around the country. Each camp involves hundreds of youth and youth leaders.

Through Workcamp, we spend a week repairing, painting, and weatherizing homes for people trapped in poverty. Home repair projects include siding, roofing, replacing windows or doors, replacing stairs, and painting.

The primary goal of Workcamp is to help young people grow in their faith while they serve. By the end of the week, kids know that they can make a difference!

Ministry in a Shelter

Our middle-school and high-school youth thoroughly enjoy playing with younger children. During the summer, we organize activities for children living in a local family shelter. At first our middle-school youth didn't understand what a shelter was or how children happened to be there. If you bring your youth to volunteer at a shelter, help them understand that a shelter provides safety for people who have nowhere else to go.

Promoting the Rights of All

1. Arrange a youth mission trip. Plan to spend a week away from home helping residents trapped in poverty. Projects could include painting, replacing doors and windows, roofing, and repairing foundations. Group Workcamps offers summer mission experiences for church youth groups. For more information call 1.888.761.6616 or go to groupmissiontrips.com.

2. Get involved with Habitat for Humanity. For more information on how to volunteer with Habitat, go to habitat.org.

3. Organize a "Random Acts of Kindness" day. Offer to help older parishioners with yard cleanup in the spring and fall. Although most seniors are able to live independently, tasks such as raking and trimming bushes can be too difficult. Advertise your free labor in the parish bulletin. In addition, your pastor or pastoral minister can help identify people in need. Be sure to include those who are recently widowed.

4. Encourage youth to participate in an urban immersion retreat. These experiences help raise awareness of various urban issues as well as agencies that serve lower income families and people in need. Contact your diocesan Youth Ministry or Social Justice Office to learn about opportunities in your area.

5. Organize a paint-a-thon. Spend a weekend painting a home for someone in need. Ask local hardware and paint stores to donate materials. Your pastor or pastoral minister can identify those who could benefit from this project.

6. Host a speaker from DignityUSA to address the need for respect and justice for people of all sexual orientation. Promote the need and the responsibility to be welcoming and respecting of all persons no matter their sexual orientation.

7. Contact your local chapter of the American Red Cross (redcross.org) about organizing or hosting a blood drive. Many volunteers will be needed for a variety of tasks, including setting up the site, welcoming donors, taking donor information, and providing juice and cookies.

8. Help low-income families plant and tend flower or vegetable gardens. Ask parishioners and local nurseries to donate supplies or to provide supplies at a discounted price.

9. Set up a mentorship program in your parish. Pair older children with younger children who can benefit from some special attention. A commitment of about three hours a month is appropriate. Mentors can help young children with homework or invite young children to community events.

10. Contact your parish social justice minister or contact your diocesan Social Justice or Catholic Charities office to identify transitional housing facilities in your area. Organize a collection of personal care and other items currently needed by the residents. These may include toiletries, bedding, clothing, notebooks, and pens.

11. Contact a church community that has a different ethnic background than your parish. Arrange to do a service project involving youth from both communities. Your diocesan Youth Ministry Office may be able to help you locate another parish.

12. Arrange to build playground equipment in a low-income neighborhood or day-care center. Contact churches or schools in low-income areas to find out where you can help.

13. Offer to weatherize homes. Spend a day repairing windows and screens, caulking, and painting homes for people in need. Ask a local hardware store to donate materials for the project. Your pastor or pastoral minister can help identify those who can benefit from this project.

14. Organize a low-cost or free babysitting service for single parents who are in school. Advertise the service in the parish bulletin, at local high schools, technical schools, community colleges,

and colleges. Be sure to follow all parish and school child safety policies.

15. Contact your parish social justice minister or your diocesan Social Justice or Catholic Charities office to identify family shelters in your area. Arrange to host activities at the shelter. Plan a few hours of organized games, crafts, treats, and other festivities.

16. Collect multicultural toys, books, and dolls to donate to a child-care center.

17. Develop a drama team to do a presentation on racism and other forms of prejudice. Offer to present the drama to other churches in your community.

18. Contact your diocesan Mission Office to find about making donations of sacramentals and other religious items to Third World countries or to missions sponsored by your parish or diocese.

19. Also contact your diocesan Mission Office to find out ways that children and youth can support the missionary efforts of your diocese.

20. Go to Catholic Campaign for Human Development (usccb.org) and povertyusa.org to find out about the Catholic Church's work to eliminate poverty and to promote social justice in the United States.

CHAPTER 7

CARE FOR CREATION

" The Catholic tradition insists that we show our respect for the Creator by our stewardship of creation. Care for the earth . . . is a requirement of our faith (*Sharing Catholic Social Teaching: Challenges and Directions* 6). **"**

Opportunities for caring for creation are as abundant and various as God's creations themselves. Whether you are looking for a large or small, local or global, long-term or short-term project, there is a stewardship project to suit your group.

Caring for Creation

Our local school district adopted a section of highway. Since school is not in session throughout the summer, area youth groups pitch in and take care of the highway for a few months.

Our local nature center offers a variety of volunteer opportunities for youth. Sometimes we replenish the supply of wood chips on the trails and pick up litter. Other times we plant trees or help with groups of small children.

Our youth help tend gardens in the city parks. When we work together, we can quickly weed a large area. We enjoy chatting while we work. Time flies and suddenly gardening is no longer a back-breaking chore.

Ways to Care for Creation

1. Arrange to spend a weekend at a co-op or organic farm. Plan to help with chores as well as take time to learn about the environmental benefits of co-op and organic farming.

2. Encourage car pools for parish and school youth activities. Set up a carpool database to facilitate carpooling in neighborhoods. Invite young people to keep track of the results of the carpools, such as gallons of gas saved and the effect on the environment. Print the results on the parish or school Web site or in the parish or school newsletter.

3. Research and write articles for the parish and school Web sites and newsletters about how to protect the environment. Be sure to find out article length and article deadlines well in advance.

4. Arrange to plant bulbs or flowers at church, at school, at a cemetery, or elsewhere in the community. Ask a local nursery to donate plants or provide them at a reduced cost. Be sure to maintain the flowers throughout the season.

5. Arrange to plant trees. Schools, parks, churches, and other nonprofit organizations could benefit from this project.

6. Organize a recycling program in your parish. Provide containers and label them. Also be sure to arrange regular collection times.

7. Pick up litter at area parks, schools, playgrounds, and other public areas.

8. Offer a pet-care class at church for young children. Older children can share their expertise. You might consider inviting a veterinarian or Humane Society volunteer to lead the class.

9. Arrange to host a Blessing of Animals in your parish. Invite people of all ages to bring their pets to be blessed on the Feast of Saint Francis of Assisi on October 4.

10. Offer to play with a pet in your neighborhood. Pets need exercise and attention to thrive. Find out if there is a pet in your neighborhood who could benefit from a walk or some extra attention.

11. Offer to help with animal migration. As we develop more and more of our land and pollute our waters, we can inhibit animal migratory patterns. Contact your local or state parks and recreation department to learn about volunteer opportunities.

12. Garden for a neighbor. Plant and care for a flower garden for an elderly or single-parent neighbor. Your kindness will bring cheer to them every day!

13. Organize a Christmas tree recycling program. Contact your local recycling center or city parks and recreation department for information.

14. Contact your local parks department or school principal to inquire about the need for trash cans or recycling containers. Host a fundraiser and use the monies to donate these items to your school or local parks department.

15. Plant and tend flower gardens at a nursing home. The residents will enjoy the flowers when they sit outside.

16. Offer to help at a nature center. Most nature centers rely on volunteers to greet guests, maintain trails, and keep grounds clean.

17. Volunteer at a wildlife refuge. Learn about animals while you work to protect them.

18. Research volunteer opportunities at your local Humane Society. Learn more about their work at humanesociety.org.

19. Participate in Earth Day, a national day set aside for cleaning up and caring for creation. Choose Earth Day, April 24, to carry out stewardship projects.

20. Adopt a highway. Take responsibility for maintaining a section of highway in your community. For more information contact your State Department of Transportation.

21. Adopt a rainforest. One way we can save the rainforests is to purchase rain forest lands an acre at a time. To learn more about the rainforest or to purchase an acre go to rainforest-alliance.org.

22. Take responsibility for keeping a section of a river clean. Ask local disposal companies to remove the trash you collect for free. For more information on saving our rivers, visit the Web site of National River Cleanup at americanrivers.org.

23. Adopt a whale. You will receive the name and a picture of your whale immediately. As your whale is sighted over the years, you will receive updates. For more information, contact the Pacific Whale Foundation Web site at pacificwhale.org.

CHAPTER 8

PEACE

Bringing peace was essential to Jesus' ministry on Earth. As Catholics, we are called to continue Jesus' ministry of peace. We must take a firm stand against violence and hatred in our world.

> "Blessed are the peacemakers,
> for they will be called children of God"

Matthew 5:9

Peace Poles

A Peace Pole is an international symbol of peace. It is a four- or six-sided monument. Each side displays the phrase, "May Peace Prevail On Earth" in different languages.

Our youth group raised funds to purchase a Peace Pole. We planted it in the center of our church yard and surrounded it with a small flower garden. We dedicated our Peace Pole in memory of a parishioner who served our parish for many years as an advocate for youth.

Peace Be With You

1. Organize activities for children at a family shelter. Activities could include tutoring, crafts, games, sports, or reading books. To locate a shelter near you, contact your parish minister of social justice or your diocesan Catholic Charities or Social Justice office.

2. Brainstorm with the youth ways in which you can live peacemaking lives. Put the ideas into the form of a pledge. Invite all members of the group to sign and commit to keeping the pledge. Post the pledge and invite all parish members to join the youth in living as peacemakers.

3. Organize a neighborhood block party. Invite all the neighbors to gather outside for an evening to get to know one another. Lead games for the children. Consider taking pictures of each household and making a neighborhood directory.

4. Set up a peer mediation program. Train youth as peer mediators. Be sure to utilize the peer mediators for conflict resolution with their peers at parish programs. Contact your parish youth minister or school counselor for more information on peer mediation training materials.

5. Invite young people to research and write articles about violence-related issues for the parish and school Web sites and newsletters. Topics might include: gun violence; violence portrayed in music lyrics; violence portrayed in digital games, movies, and on TV; violence caused by drug and alcohol abuse; pornography and human trafficking; and bullying and cyber-bullying.

6. Participate in efforts to help alleviate suffering in countries affected by war. Contact Catholic Relief Services (crs.org) or the American Red Cross (redcross.org) for more information.

7. Raise funds for and plant a Peace Pole as a reminder to your community to live as peacemakers. To learn more about the Peace Pole Project or to order a peace pole, go to peacepoleproject.org.

CHAPTER 9

FUNDRAISING

Occasionally you may need to raise money to fund your service projects. This chapter describes a number of fundraising ideas that also provide a service to the parish and community.

Fundraisers

Our high-school youth sponsor two parties a year for middle-schoolers to raise money for the summer mission trip. In the fall, we host a dance and haunted house. Each high-schooler takes responsibility for a specific piece of the event. Some are DJs, others make scary scenes inside the haunted house, and some run the snack bar. The middle-schoolers liked the haunted house so much that many paid to go through it two or three times!

In the spring, we host a dance and an indoor eighteen-hole miniature golf course. Pairs of high-schoolers design golf holes, and each hole has a theme. Themes included sports, the '50s, Hawaii, and Barbie. Learn from our experience and try not to make the holes too difficult. The middle-schoolers like the holes they can play in 4–5 shots with the best scenery.

Additional Ideas

1. Hold a car wash. Instead of charging a fixed price, ask for donations.

2. Organize a garage sale. Invite the entire parish to donate items for the sale. You will be raising money while you provide people with an opportunity to purchase items at a lesser cost.

3. Host a pancake breakfast on a Sunday morning. You will be helping to build community in your parish while you raise money for a worthwhile cause.

4. Host a spaghetti dinner. Almost everybody likes spaghetti, and it is easy to make for large groups of people.

5. Host a Valentine dinner. Consider offering child care or activities for children so that parents can have a chance to sit and talk with each other.

6. Host a Friday night fish fry during Lent.

7. Sell poinsettias for Christmas and Easter lilies for Easter. This fundraiser provides people with an opportunity to support the youth and a convenient way to purchase their holiday plant at church.

8. Hold a bake sale after Mass. Ask youth to bake. In addition, invite all parishioners to donate goodies for the sale. Homemade items are a special treat. Consider scheduling the bake sale near a holiday like Valentine's Day or Mothers' Day and decorate treats for the occasion.

9. Team up with area chefs to plan and host a spectacular dinner. The chefs can help the young people choose a menu and teach them how to prepare and serve the meal. The dinner builds community, raises funds for youth programs, and gives chefs an opportunity to introduce young people to the culinary arts.

10. Arrange to work a concession booth. Many professional teams' stadiums utilize non-profit volunteers in their food services. The organization that the volunteers represent is paid for each volunteer. Call your local stadium for more information.

11. Arrange to bag and carry groceries. Many grocers are willing to pay for extra help during busy times of the year, such as before Thanksgiving and Christmas. You will make a hectic time of the year better for the store and its customers while earning money for youth projects.

12. Organize and advertise a "Hire a Hand" program in your parish. Many parishioners are willing to pay for a little extra help around their homes and yards. This service can supply those looking for help with hard-working, reliable assistance.

13. If you can, find a donor who will match contributions up to a certain amount. Matching contributions may encourage more people to donate, since their contribution will be doubled.

14. Provide sponsorship opportunities. Sometimes people prefer to donate money rather than purchase an item or service. Give people a vehicle for making financial contributions to youth participants.

15. Publish a list of materials that you need. For example, you may need painting supplies and caulking guns for a mission trip. Both businesses and individuals may donate what you need. Remember that people will not know what you need unless you ask.

16. When you near the end of a fund drive, publish the amount you still need to reach your goal. The information may encourage people who have been thinking about donating to act.

17. Sell religious gifts. Bring a vendor to your parish to sell crosses, books, and other religious gift items. Arrange for a percentage of the sales to go towards funding our service project. A good time of year for this sale is shortly before the celebration of First Holy Communion or Confirmation.

18. Sponsor an evening at a fast-food restaurant. Some fast-food restaurants will specify an evening for a nonprofit organization. A portion of the sales will go to the organization. All you need to do is encourage people to eat at that restaurant on your specific night.

19. Have high-school youth host special events for junior-high or middle-school youth. Possible events might include dances, a haunted house, or an indoor mini-golf course.

20. Organize kids' carnival games at a community or parish festival. These games are simple and can be staffed by children of all ages with adult supervision.

CHAPTER 10

DOS AND DON'TS

- Do plan time for preparation before and debrief afterward.

- Do stress and maintain confidentiality. You need to protect both the children and the people you serve.

- Do involve young people in the decision-making process as you choose service projects.

- Do take time to visit with those you serve. Some people, especially the elderly, may be lonely and will appreciate the company.

- Do offer the same opportunities to both boys and girls. Don't discriminate.

- Do make both your own and the agency's expectations clear.

- Do follow all agency guidelines regarding adult-to-child ratios, attire restrictions, age restrictions, and behavior expectations.

- Do give good directions to the facility. Don't waste time lost in traffic.

- Do make sure that all volunteers will be utilized. Don't have some young people simply watching while others are busy serving.

- Do make sure sure that the purpose of the project is well defined. Discuss with young people the effect the ministry will have on those they serve.

- Do help the young people recognize that when they serve, they also receive.

- Do discourage unnecessary complaints. Both positive and negative attitudes are contagious. Help the young people understand that it is a privilege to have an opportunity to share their gifts with others.

- Do discourage the young people from judging those they serve. Compassion involves putting ourselves in someone else's place and understanding their circumstances. We are called to serve with compassion, not judge.

- Do support and empower young people as they learn to serve and expand their comfort zone.

- Don't make service a requirement to be completed outside of program time. Instead, integrate service into the religious education program so that young people can learn about the importance of service. Then, invite and inspire young people to get more involved in living their life of faith in service to others.

- Do avoid projects that are simply busy work with no real effect.

- Do provide an opportunity for young people to share their service project experience with their families and the parish community. Culminate a project with a potluck supper, slides, and a chance for young people to share their stories.

- Don't allow people to take advantage of young people. Don't let your youth get involved in a project that is so horrendous no one else would do it.

- Do find people with the skills and gifts you need and utilize them in the program. For example, you may need people to teach youth about the elderly or how to repair a window. You may need drivers and cooks. Remember, the adults who assist you with service projects provide a powerful example to the young volunteers. The more opportunities you provide, the more people of faith the youngsters will come to know.

- Do provide every opportunity you can to invite and allow all parishioners to support young people and their service projects.

Agencies, Organizations, and Offices

1. Every diocese has a Catholic Charities office. To find the office in your area, go to catholiccharitiesusa.org.

2. Catholic Relief Services responds to major emergencies and assists the poor and vulnerable overseas. For more information, go to crs.org.

3. The American Red Cross provides disaster relief and emergency supplies in the aftermath of disasters. The American Red Cross also organizes blood, organ, bone marrow, and tissue donations. For more information, go to redcross.org.

4. Call your local school principal or school district office to find opportunities for volunteer service.

5. Call city offices to find out how to get youth involved in community service experiences. Your community may need assistance with parks, beaches, festivals, landscaping, and gardening.

6. Call county offices for information about service opportunities for youth. The county may also need assistance with parks, beaches, special events, landscaping, and gardening.

7. The local community counseling center will be aware of agencies in your area where you can serve, such as shelters and transitional housing.

8. Call the volunteer coordinator at local nursing homes and care facilities to offer your services.

9. Special Olympics offers athletic training and competition for children and adults with intellectual disabilities. For more information on the Special Olympics and ways to volunteer, go to specialolympics.org.

10. The Salvation Army provides disaster relief and emotional and spiritual support to disaster victims and first responders. For more information, go to salvationarmyusa.org.

11. Feeding America coordinates a nationwide network of food banks in the effort to end hunger in America. For more information, go to feedingamerica.org.

12. Oxfam International is committed to respecting human rights and helping people lift themselves out of poverty. The organization is currently active in over 90 countries around the world. For more information, go to oxfam.org.

13. Heifer International invites donors to contribute toward the purchase of farm animals for families in poverty. This helps families achieve a sustainable source of income and food. For more information, go to heifer.org.

14. The United States Department of Labor works to assure fair, safe, and healthy working conditions for all workers. To learn more about the work of this government agency, go to dol.gov.

15. Group Mission Trips hosts Group Workcamps that offer summer mission trip experiences around the country for church youth groups. For more information, go to groupmissiontrips.com.

16. Habitat for Humanity is a Christian organization committed to providing housing for low-income families. For more information, go to habitat.org.

Notes

Notes

Notes

CPSIA information can be obtained
at www.ICGtesting.com
Printed in the USA
JSHW011228021020
8446JS00007B/115